# Images of Hawaii's Flowers:

## A Pictorial Guide to the Aloha State's Flowering Plants

Photography
by
Loye Guthrie, John Mertus,
JoeCo Photography,
and HSI Stock

Contributions
by
Loye Guthrie
Wendy Carter Ford
and Jean Guthrie

This publication is a copyrighted product ⓒ1996 Hawaiian Service, Inc.
94-535 Uke`e Street, Waipahu, Hawaii 96797-4214
Telephone (808) 676-5026 • FAX (808) 676-5156
Any reproduction of all or part of this publication is prohibited without written
permission of the publisher.
ISBN: 0-930492-59-5
10 9 8 7 6 5 4 3 2 1
Printed in Australia

# Index of Flowers

# Index of Flowers

# AFRICAN TULIP TREE

*Spathodea campanulata*

### Flame of the Forest

These very tall trees produce flaming, tulip-like flowers, the skirts of which are hemmed with a brilliant gold fluting. They emerge from two-inch-long green pods shaped like tiny bananas. Natives of tropical Africa, they can be easily found on all the islands, blooming year round.

# ALLAMANDA

*Allamanda cathartica*

Lani Ali`i

Bearing fragrant yellow cups approximately four to six inches in diameter, the Allamanda loves a moist climate and cool weather. Allamanda is a member of the periwinkle family originally from Brazil. Gardens lining the road to Mt. Tantalus on Oahu are a good place to see them.

## ANGEL'S TRUMPET

*Datura candida*

### Nana Honua

These eight-to nine-inch-long flowers seem to be hanging upside down on their tall bushes. The leaves and flowers are both poisonous if ingested. These beautiful plants, originally from tropical America, can be found on Mt.Tantalus and at Foster Gardens on Oahu.

# ANTHURIUM

*Anthurium andraeanum*

### Flamingo Flower

A member of the arum family, the anthurium is related to such well-known plants as: calla lily, dieffenbachia, philodendron, and monstera. In Hawaii, it can be found growing in many home gardens. Anthuriums are cultivated for their unusual and popular cut flowers.

# ANTHURIUM

*Anthurium andraeanum*

Flamingo Flower

Shiny and waxy, anthuriums come in many colors: green, white, pink, orange, and brown, but red is the most popular. Many anthurium farms, along the volcano highway on the Big Island, offer easy viewing of anthuriums as they grow in the shade of large hapu`u tree ferns.

# ANTHURIUM

*Anthurium andraeanum*

Flamingo Flower

There are over 500 species of anthurium all from tropical America. Flowers can last for months on the plant and for weeks when cut. The cut flowers are sold in most Hawaiian florist shops as well as at the Hawaii airports for transport to mainland and foreign destinations.

# BANANA

*Musa paradisiaca*

Mai`a

Growing on a stem from the top of the trunk, the banana's purple petals fall off as the flowers beneath begin to develop into the green, then yellow, fruit. The species, originally from India, is now found growing wild in Hawaii, in home gardens, and cultivated on farms.

# BE-STILL, YELLOW OLEANDER

*Thevetia peruviana*

Noho-Malie

All parts of this large bush or small tree, on which the Be-still flower clusters grow, are poisonous. In spite of its name, it is related to the periwinkle family, not the oleander. This plant can be seen along many of Hawaii's highways as it makes an attractive, easy-to-grow hedge.

# BIRD-OF-PARADISE

*Strelitzia reginae*

### Cranes-bill

As one of nature's most unusual blooms, the Bird-of-Paradise can be seen on all the islands of Hawaii. It is a hardy, long lasting plant whose cut flowers can last for weeks. Originally from South Africa, this plant is a member of the banana family.

# BOUGAINVILLEA

*Bougainvillea spectabilis*

## Pukanawila

This versatile flower grows sometimes as high as twelve to fifteen feet on thorny bushes and vines. Bougainvillea appears in a wide range of colors. First found in Rio de Janeiro, Brazil, by French navigator Louis A. de Bougainville, it is now seen all over Hawaii.

# BOTTLE BRUSH

*Callistemon linearis*

### Myrtle family

These bright red, brush-like flowers give this plant its name. Almost every neighborhood includes these graceful, decorative trees. An Australian shrub or small tree 12 - 30 feet tall, it is related to the guava, mountain apple, and `ohia trees.

# BROMELIAD

*Aechmea mooreana*

## Pineapple family

There are more than 2,500 known species of bromeliads. They are becoming more and more popular because of their easy care. They can be seen in Hawaii's botanical gardens, and they are often used by landscapers for hotels and shopping centers throughout Hawaii.

# BROMELIAD

*Guzmania lingulata, minor*

## Pineapple family

More than 50 species distributed from southern Brazil to Mexico are now grown in Hawaiian gardens. Related to the pineapple, bromeliads have a spike -like flower that grows out of the colorful leaves. They can be found in many gift shops, packaged for export.

# CALATHEA

*Calathea burle-marxii*

### Ice Blue

Usually grown for their distinctive, ornamental patterned leaves, many calathea also have beautifully unusual flowers. Part of the arrowroot family from tropical America, they are found only in the damp rainy areas of the islands.

# CANNA LILY

*Canna indica*

Ali`ipoe

This useful plant is often seen growing wild on Hawaiian roadsides. The flowers range from pale yellow to a dark red, with seeds that are used for lei necklaces and in gourd calabashes for hula rattles. A native of tropical America, it is now found in most tropical areas of the world.

# CHENILLE

*Acalypha hispida*

A native of the East Indies, this plant can be seen as a medium-sized hedge or as a beautiful hanging-basket house plant. It is easily identified by its long red, velvety flowers which can reach 18 inches. It can be found at Foster Gardens and Waimea Falls on Oahu.

# CUP OF GOLD

*Solandra hartwegii*

### Golden Cup

Originally from the West Indies, the cup of gold is a member of the potato family. It can be found on Mt. Tantalus, which is only a few minutes drive from downtown Honolulu. It has very large, white to dark yellow blossoms and grows on vines up to sixty feet long in the forest areas.

# DWARF POINCIANA

*Caesalpinia pulcherrima*

`Ohai-ali`i

Sometimes called the peacock flower or Pride of Barbados, this beautiful flowering bush or small tree is often used as a hedge in Hawaii. The flowers resemble those of the royal poinciana tree, though they are smaller with longer stamens.

# FUCHSIA

*Fuchsia magellanica*

Kulapepeiao

An ornamental shrub from South America, fuchsia has gone wild in Hawaii's forests. The Hawaiian name means "earring' as the flowers are small and beautiful like earrings. They can be seen at Hawaii Volcanoes National Park on Hawaii or Poli Poli Park on Maui.

# GINGER, KAHILI

*Hedychium gardnerianum*
`Awapuhi

Originally from the Himalayas, this fragrant flower can reach a height of six feet. It is seen in many Hawaiian gardens and found growing wild on most islands, noticeably in the Kula area of Maui. The name "Kahili" came from the resemblance to a king's feathered kahili staff.

# GINGER, RED
*Alpinia purpurata*
`Awapuhi-`ula`ula

The bright red blooms at the end of the leafstalk are actually the bracts (colored leaves). The true flowers are small and white and appear inside the base of the red bracts. They can be found in many island landscapes, as well as in nearly every Hawaiian florist shop.

# GINGER, SHELL
*Alpinia speciosa*
`Awapuhi-luhe luhe

Originally from tropical East Asia, shell ginger can now be found in most damp areas of the Hawaiian islands. It has a delicate spicy fragrance and is sometimes used in flower arrangements, although it does not last as long as the red ginger.

# GINGER, TORCH

*Phaeomeria magnifica*

`Awapuhi-ko`oko`o

These giant flowers are surrounded by green bamboo-like stalks which grow up to sixteen-feet-tall. The bloom itself stands on a long stem of about six feet. This plant originated in the East Indies and may be seen in most of Hawaii's botanical gardens.

# GINGER, WHITE

*Hedychium coronarium*
`Awapuhi-ke`oke`o

Originally from India, this ginger is the most popular in the use of lei making because of its wonderful fragrance. White and yellow ginger can be seen growing wild on many Hawaiian roadsides such as: Volcano Highway, Hawaii; Hana Highway, Maui; and Tantalus Road, Oahu.

# HELICONIA, CHARTACEA

*Heliconia chartacea, Lane ex Barreiros*

Sexy Pink

Sexy Pink is a pendent or hanging heliconia. Originally distributed from Guianas to the Amazon Basin, it is now cultivated in Hawaii, Florida, Barbados, and Costa Rica for its beautiful, long-lasting flowers. It can be seen at the University of Hawaii's Lyon Arboretum on Oahu.

# HELICONIA, SASSY

*Heliconia psittacorum*

### Suriname Sassy

Sassy blooms all year long (most prolific in April through November) so it is seen in many private gardens as well as in resort landscapes and flower farms. Originally from Costa Rica, it is now grown in most tropical areas of the world and is used in flower arrangements.

# HELICONIA, RUIZ & PAVON

*Heliconia rostrata*

## Rostrata

Originally from Amazonian Peru and Ecuador, rostrata is now found widely-cultivated around the world. Its beautiful, long-lasting flowers are popular with florists. It can be found in most of Hawaii's tropical botanical gardens.

# HELICONIA, SCHNEANA

*Heliconia bihai*

Lobster Claw

Schneana was originally from northern South America, but it can now be found in most tropical areas. The large, erect flowers are popular with florists and are now widely cultivated. They can be seen growing wild on Hawaiian roadsides as well as in tropical botanical gardens.

## HIBISCUS, CHINESE

*Hibiscus rosa- sinensis*

### Aloalo lahilahi

The now most common red hibiscus was made the official territorial flower of Hawaii in 1923. Found all over the islands and often seen used for hedges, this plant can grow to a height of 20 feet. Crushed flowers were used as a purple dye for the hair and as an aid to digestion.

# HIBISCUS, HAU

*Hibiscus tiliaceus*

### Cotton family

The hau, was very important to ancient Hawaiians. Its wood was used for the outriggers on canoes, and its bark fiber was woven into ropes and net bags. The most famous hau plant grows on the lanai of the Halekulani Hotel at the ocean end of Lewers Street in Waikiki.

# HIBISCUS WAIMEAE

*Hibiscus waimeae*

Koki`o-ke`oke`o

One of many native Hawaiian hibiscus is the beautiful white H. waimeae which grows on the steep, cliffs of Waimea Canyon, Kauai. The trees, which attain a height of 18 to 30 feet, can be seen on the trail below Waipo`o Falls. The flowers bloom during the summer and fall and have a light fragrance.

# HIBISCUS, WHITE

*Hibiscus hybrid*

### Aloalo pupupu

There are 80 genera and 1000 species of hibiscus, including many native Hawaiian species. Its colors are equally varied, but red, yellow, and white are most commonly found in Hawaii. Hula dancers often wear them in their hair during performances.

# HIBISCUS, YELLOW
*Hibiscus hybrid*
## Aloalo lahilahi

Hibiscus in Hawaii have come from such diverse places as India, Australia, South America, Philippines, Africa, and China. Picked flowers will last all day without water, and so they are found displayed on many counters of stores and banks throughout Hawaii.

# HILO HOLLY

*Ardisia crispa*

### Kolea

Hawaiians used the red sap of Hilo Holly as a dye for their tapa cloth and mats. It is native to India, China, and the East Indies. The short shrub can be seen in the native forests and along roadsides. The berries are edible but lack any real flavor, though they are popular with birds.

# HONG KONG ORCHID

*Bauhinia blakeana*

## St. Thomas Tree

Orchid trees were originally from tropical India, China, Africa, and Southeast Asia. The fragrant blossoms bloom from October through May in Hawaii, and many varieties can be found in family gardens as well as park and resort landscapes.

# RED JADE VINE

*Strongylodon lucidus*

Nuku`i`iwi

The red jade vine is originally from New Guinea and is rare in Hawaii. There is a blue jade vine (Strongylodon macrobotrys ) from the Phillipines which is more commonly seen in Hawaii's gardens. Both are used to make spectacular leis, though they may stain clothes.

# LEHUA HAOLE

*Calliandra inaequilatera*

## False Lehua

Lehua Haole is a member of the legume (or bean) family and the mimosa subfamily, which includes monkeypod, koa, and ohi`a trees. A small shrub native to Bolivia, it is used in Hawaii for leis and is found in many Hawaiian gardens.

# LIPSTICK TREE

*Bixa orellana*

`Alaea

The lipstick tree is originally from the Amazon region. After flowering, the dark red pods dry and split open, revealing deep red seeds. The seeds are waxy and produce a dye that was once used in lipstick, cheeses, butter, and margarine. It is now seen in gardens as an ornamental plant.

# MEXICAN CREEPER

*Antigonon leptopus*

## Mountain Rose

This wild climbing vine can be found on many hillsides and cliffs throughout Hawaii, such as in Honolulu and Kaanapali. It flowers most of the year and prefers hot climates like its native Mexico. The roots or tubers can weigh as much as 15 pounds and are edible.

# NIGHT-BLOOMING CEREUS

*Hylocereus undatus*

Pa-nini-o-kapuna-hou

This unusual climbing cactus produces giant, one-foot-wide flowers, which bloom only at night from June to November. The plant has a fruit that is rare, but deliciously refreshing. A spectacular hedge runs a quarter-mile along the border of Punahou School on Oahu.

# `OHI`A-LEHUA

*Metrosideros polymorpha*

`Ohia

This is the most common tree in Hawaii's native forests. Found on all the main islands, except Niihau and Kahoolawe, this species provides abundant nectar to many types of native Hawaiian honeycreeper. A great place to view `ohi`a trees is at Hakalau National Wildlife Refuge on Hawaii.

# ORCHID, CATTLEYA

*Brassolaeliocattleya*

`Okika

The orchid family is the second largest family of flowering plants with more than 600 genera and more than 12,000 species. Most tropical species grow on trees in the wild. There are beautiful examples to be seen at Foster Gardens on Oahu, as well as at most garden shops around the islands.

# ORCHID, DENDROBIUM

*Dendrobium nobile*

`Okika

Orchids are found in a large number of Hawaiian gardens. They can be found growing in pots or hanging baskets, out of the ground and in trees. Many species have a deep, musky fragrance which is used as a base for many popular perfumes.

# ORCHID, PHALENOPSIS

*Phalenopsis gallant beau*

`Okika

Commercial orchid growing exploded between 1900 and 1920 because of the demand for unusual and beautiful flowers and plants. Today it is a multi-million dollar business with growers throughout the world. The vanilla bean is the only edible product of the orchid species.

# ORCHID, VANDA

*Vanda suavis*

`Okika

Vandas are often used as decoration on Hawaiian drinks and food plates. One imported orchid species known as bamboo orchid has gone wild on the island of Hawaii, thus giving the island the nickname of the "Orchid Isle." These can be seen growing along the volcano highway.

# ORCHID, ONCIDIUM

*Oncidium blue monarch*

`Okika

Oncidium is one of the largest and most popular of the orchid genera. From tropical America, most were epiphytic, growing on trees in their natural habitat. Oncidium are now grown in many Hawaiian gardens for their many-flowered, colorful sprays.

# PAPAYA

*Carica papaya*

He`i

A native of tropical America, these trees grow 5-to 25-feet-tall. Leaves grow from the hollow trunk, with flowers appearing at the base of the stems. The flowers are fragrant and quickly ripen into the mature papaya fruit. There are numerous papaya farms in the Puna District of Hawaii.

# PINEAPPLE

*Ananas comosus*

### Hala-kahiki

Originating in Brazil, pineapple is believed to have been in Hawaii since 1813. Each fruit consists of many six-sided berries forming rows around the fruit. The flowers, one to each of these berries, are blueish and less than 0.5-inch-long. There are vast pineapple fields on Oahu and Maui.

# PLUMERIA, SINGAPORE

*Plumeria obtusa*

Melia

The bright white flowers of the Singapore plumeria are seen all over the Hawaiian islands. These fragrant blossoms have a wonderful scent, but they are not usually used for leis because they are quick to wilt. The Singapore plumeria does not lose its leaves in winter as do other plumerias.

# PLUMERIA, RED

*Plumeria rubra*

### Melia

Plumerias are part of the periwinkle family found in most tropical regions of the world. Their fragrant flowers are most popularly used for leis. They are found in many graveyards around Hawaii and are sometimes referred to as "Temple Flowers."

# POINSETTIA
*Euphorbia pulcherrima*
### Christmas flower

A native of Mexico, poinsettia have become known as the "Christmas flower" around the world. In Hawaii, there are roadside hedges 12-feet-high displaying their bright colors between November and March. Poinsettia bears bright red floral leaves; other varieties boast pink, white, yellow or cream.

# PROTEA, DUCHESS

*Protea eximia*

### Pink-spoon

Originally from South Africa and Australia, protea are now being widely grown in Hawaii for their long-lasting, unusual flowers. They vary from small shrubs to tall trees, with hundreds of flowers on each plant. There are protea farms in upcountry Maui and in the Waimea area of Hawaii.

# PROTEA

*Banksia and Protea*

Frost, Pincushion and Pink Mink (L to R)

Protea bloom year-round and are found in the higher elevations of Maui and Hawaii. They have become a big business in the Hawaii cut-flower trade, as the fresh flowers can last for a month or more. They can be dried for even longer-lasting arrangements.

# SHRIMP PLANT

*Beloperone guttata*

### Yellow shrimp

The shrimp plant can be seen as a ground cover in many of Hawaii's gardens. Originally from Mexico, its colors may vary from white to yellow, orange, and red. The true flowers are small and white, emerging from the colored tubular bracts.

# SILVERSWORD

*Argyroxiphium sandwicense*

### `Ahinahina

The silversword, one of Hawaii's strangest plants, is endemic to high (6,000 to 12,000 ft.) volcanic areas. It takes from 9 to 14 years for the plant to blossom. Its six-foot-tall stalk bears many small flower heads, which resemble its sunflower relative. It is found at Haleakala National Park on Maui.

# STEPHANOTIS

*Stephanotis floribunda*

Pua-male

Blooming April through October, the flowers are often used in wedding bouquets and leis. The vine, growing 15 feet high or more, was originally from Madagascar. It is seen growing on fences in Hawaii, with clusters of of six to eight flowers, each with a delicate fragrance.

# TIARE O TAHITI

*Gardenia taitensis*

Nanu

A shrub from the Society Islands, this gardenia looks like a delicate white pinwheel, but it has the same wonderful fragrance as other gardenias. They can be found as hedges all over the islands and are related to the coffee plant which is also in the Rubiaceae family.

# WATER LILY
## *Nymphaeaceae*
### Lilia-lana-i-ka-wai

Originally from South America, nymphaeas can be found in most Hawaiian water gardens. The flowers are either white, red, yellow, lavender, pink, or blue. They float on top of the water and can last from one to seven days. There are some beautiful examples on Kauai.

# WOOD-ROSE

*Operculina tuberosa*

Pili-kai

After the yellow tube-like flower of the woodrose has died, it produces a fruiting capsule which contains hairy black seeds and is surrounded by five stiff, petal-like sepals. These wood-roses are used for dry bouquets and wreaths. They grow in low mountain and jungle areas of the islands.

# NOTES

# HAWAIIAN SERVICE INC.
# FAVORITES

## HAWAIIAN ISLAND BOOKS

***Informative as well as beautiful.***

Soft cover, 7 x 10, full color pictorial books

| | | |
|---|---|---|
| The Island of Maui, 32pgs. | #20009 | **$4.95** |
| The Island of Oahu, 32 pgs. | #20010 | **$4.95** |
| The Island of Kauai, 32 pgs. | #20008 | **$4.95** |
| The Island of Hawaii, 32 pgs. | #20090 | **$4.95** |
| Pearl Harbor, 32 pgs. | #20015 | **$4.95** |
| Tropical Drinks, 32 pgs. | #20080 | **$4.95** |
| Natural Hawaii, 64 pgs. | #20087 | **$7.95** |
| Beautiful Hawaiian Flowers•, 64 pgs. | #20088 | **$7.95** |
| Flowering Trees of Hawaii•, 64 pgs. | #20089 | **$7.95** |

• *New titles available summer 1996*

## ISLANDS OF HAWAII BOOK

***Our Number One selling book.***
Visit all the islands with this beautiful, 8 1/2 x 11", 64 page, perfect bound book of the Hawaiian Islands. Includes full color images from the islands of Hawaii, Kauai, Oahu, Molokai & Maui.

**Islands of Hawaii     #20007 $8.95**

## HAWAIIAN COLORING BOOKS

***A perfect gift for children everywhere.***
Enjoy the fun of coloring & share the Hawaiian stories in words, pictures & adventures with Hawaiian Service's collection of coloring books.

| | | |
|---|---|---|
| Hawaiian Gecko | #20083 | **$5.95** |
| Hawaii's Favorite Fish | #20085 | **$5.95** |
| Hawaiian Kids, Parade | #20036 | **$5.95** |
| Hawaiian Kids, Hula | #20037 | **$5.95** |

## Mail Orders to:
**HAWAIIAN SERVICE, INC. 94-535 Uke`e Street, Suite 100, Waipahu, Hawaii 96797-4212**

# ORDER TOLL FREE 1-800-626-5285

## SHIPPING & HANDLING

| ORDERS | USA | FOREIGN | ORDERS | USA | FOREIGN |
|---|---|---|---|---|---|
| $10.00 & UNDER | $1.95 | $3.95 | $50.01- $75.00 | $9.95 | $19.95 |
| $10.01 - $25.00 | $4.95 | $9.95 | $75.01 - $100.00 | $13.95 | $27.95 |
| $25.01 - $50 .00 | $7.95 | $15.95 | $100.01 - $150.00 | $16.95 | $33.95 |

PRICE BASED ON DELIVERY TO ONE ADDRESS
**ALLOW 4-6 WEEKS FOR DELIVERY**

If a particular book you order is out of stock, we will replace it with another one unless you direct us otherwise.